WELCOME TO 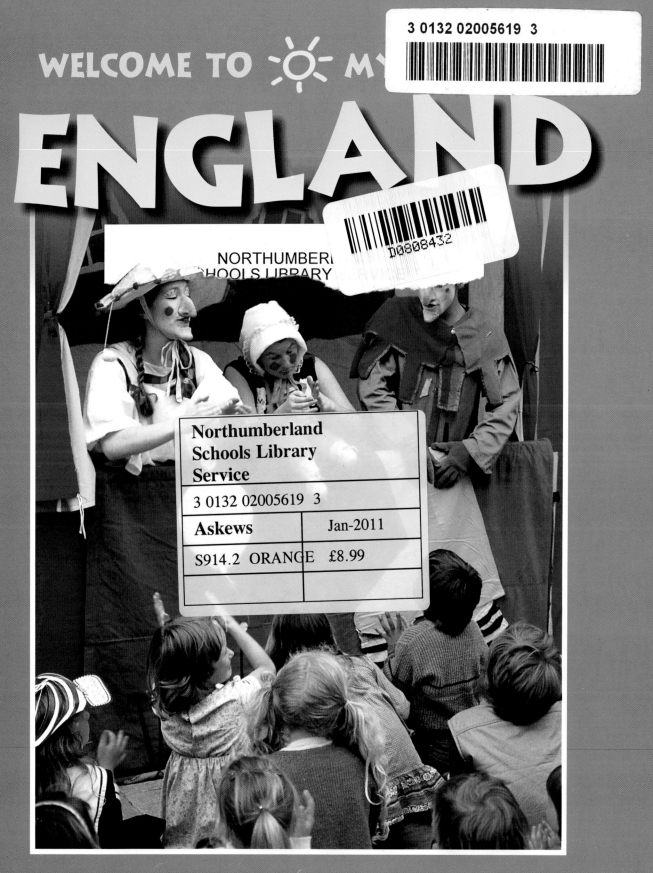 MY
ENGLAND

FRANKLIN WATTS
LONDON·SYDNEY

Written by: Maree Lister, Marti Sevier,
Roseline Ngcheong-Lum
Editors: Cheryl Sim and Melvin Neo
Designer: Benson Tan
Photo research: Thomas Khoo

PHOTO CREDITS

Alamy/Bes Stock: 35
Alamy/Photolibrary: 3 (top), 3 (centre), 6, 7, 9 (all), 11,
    12, 15 (top), 16, 17, 19, 20, 25, 26, 27, 32, 36, 37, 39
    (bottom), 40, 41, 43, 45
Bes Stock: 2, 8
Corbis: 22
David Fowler/Shutterstock: cover
Getty Images: 15 (centre)
Hutchison Library: 3 (bottom), 30
Illustrated London News Picture Library: 13, 14, 29 (top), 33
Photolibrary: 4, 5, 10, 21, 23, 24, 29 (bottom), 31, 38
Topham Picturepoint: 1, 15 (bottom), 18, 28, 34, 39 (top)

This edition published in 2010
by Franklin Watts

Designed and originated by
Marshall Cavendish International (Asia) Pte Ltd
Copyright © Marshall Cavendish International (Asia) Pte Ltd 2010
Marshall Cavendish is a trademark of Times Publishing Limited.

Franklin Watts
338 Euston Road
London NW1 3BH

This publication represents the opinions and views of the authors
based on their personal experience, knowledge and research. The
information in this book serves as a general guide only. The authors
and publisher have used their best efforts in preparing this book
and disclaim liability rising directly and indirectly from the use and
application of this book.

Dewey number 942'.086

ISBN 978 1 4451 0204 7

Franklin Watts is a division of Hachette Children's Books,
an Hachette UK company.
www.hachette.co.uk

Printed in Malaysia

Contents

Words that appear in the glossary are printed in **boldface** type the first time they occur in the text.

The fountain at Trafalgar Square in London is popular with visitors.

Welcome to England!

England has been a world leader for hundreds of years. The English people have **invented** many things and travelled to many places. England, Scotland, Wales and Northern Ireland make up the United Kingdom. Come and visit England and the English people.

The London Eye is Europe's largest observation wheel and offers a breathtaking view of the capital as it rotates high above the ground.

The Flag of England

The flag of England has a red cross on a white background. It is called the Cross of St. George, the **patron saint** of England. The Union Jack is the flag of the United Kingdom.

The Land

England is a small country, making up about half of the area of the United Kingdom. It has a land area of 130,410 square kilometres. Its neighbours are Scotland to the north and Wales to the west. The southwestern tip of the country is called Land's End.

A farmhouse is nestled at the foot of a hill in the Cumbrian region in northern England.

Mevagissey is a village in the county of Cornwall near Land's End.

England is mostly flat, with a few mountains in the north. At 978 metres, the tallest mountain is Scafell Pike. It is located in a region called the Lake District. This region is also home to England's largest lake, Lake Windermere. The longest river is the Thames. It starts in the Cotswold hills in the west central of the country and cuts across southern England to London.

Seasons

The English climate is mild. Winters are cold but not freezing and summers are not very hot. However, the country receives substantial rainfall. It rains in some areas all year, with the wettest weather in the Lake District. In wintertime, the coast is battered by strong winds called gales.

Bright yellow daffodils announce the beginning of the spring season.

Pheasant shooting is permitted in the English countryside. Pheasant shooting is considered a sport and the catch is taken home to eat.

Plants and Animals

Green **pastures** cover most of the countryside in England. Although there are not very many forests, parks and gardens fill with colourful flowers in spring.

The largest English animal is the red deer. Other animals prowling the countryside include foxes, badgers, stoats and voles. Many species of bird can be spotted in the English skies and fish in the rivers and seas. Seals live in the shallow waters off the east coast of England.

The rose is England's national flower.

History

The earliest known people living in England were the **Celts**, who came from central Europe. In 55 BCE, the Roman emperor Julius Caesar defeated the Celts and made England part of the **Roman Empire**. Although the local tribes rebelled time and again, the Romans ruled England for nearly five hundred years. They brought Christianity to the Celts and various improvements to daily life.

During the time of the Roman Empire, these hot spring baths were used for medicinal purposes. The Romans named the town *Aquae Sulis*, or Bath.

Many legends exist about King Arthur and his group of brave knights. This round table, which he supposedly used for meetings and feasts, now hangs on a wall in Winchester Cathedral.

In 406 CE, the Romans were called back to Rome. By 600 CE, Germanic people known as Anglo-Saxons ruled England. In 1066, William the Conqueror from France became king. During the second half of the **Middle Ages** (500–1500 CE), England took part in the **Crusades**, an attempt by Christians to take back Jerusalem from the Muslims.

Queen Elizabeth I ruled England for forty-five years. She made the Anglican Church England's main religious body.

Change and Expansion

In 1534, King Henry VIII set up the **Church of England**, or Anglican Church, in place of Catholicism, which had been the state religion for over a thousand years. As head of the new church, he replaced the Catholic pope as religious leader of England. After Henry's death, Catholics and Anglicans fought for control of England. These struggles took place during the Reformation, a long period of change within Christianity.

The Duke of Wellington won many battles for England in the eighteenth century.

Henry's daughter, Queen Elizabeth I, helped expand England in the second half of the sixteenth century. During and after her reign, English explorers colonized many parts of Africa, Asia and America. The **colonies** provided great wealth for England. However, the American colonies were not happy under English rule. They proclaimed independence in 1776 and defeated the English after seven years of fighting. American independence was recognized by England in 1783.

During both world wars, many women lent their support to the troops by working in factories that produced weapons and medicines.

The Twentieth Century

England suffered great losses during the two world wars. Soldiers died fighting and major cities were bombed. After World War II, colonies such as India and Burma (present-day Myanmar) became independent. England's economy recovered after the wars. Today, England is a major partner in the **European Union** (EU) and has a strong influence on world politics.

King Henry VIII (1491-1547)

Henry VIII is famous for his six wives. His first wife could not give him a son so he wanted to remarry. As the Catholic Church did not allow this, he created the Church of England and **annulled** his marriage to his wife.

Henry VIII

William Shakespeare (1564-1616)

William Shakespeare is considered by many to be the greatest writer in the English language. He wrote many poems and plays that have been translated into different languages. Most secondary school students in English-speaking countries study Shakespeare's works.

William Shakespeare

Margaret Thatcher (1925-)

Margaret Thatcher became the first female prime minister of England in 1979. She was called the 'Iron Lady' because of her strong views and forceful manner.

Margaret Thatcher

The Government and the Economy

Government

The English style of government is called a **parliamentary monarchy**. This means that the country is governed by an elected parliament, with its king or queen as a **symbolic** head. Although Queen Elizabeth II is the ruler of the country, she has no power to make national decisions on her own.

The Trooping of the Colour is a grand parade that takes place during the queen's birthday celebration.

The Houses of Parliament are at Westminster on the bank of the River Thames in London. To the right is the famous clock tower, affectionately known as Big Ben, that was built in 1859.

The power to make decisions rests with the parliament, made up of the House of Lords and the House of Commons. Members of the latter are called members of parliament, or MPs, while those from the former are simply known as lords. Both Houses work closely together when making laws. While MPs are elected by the public, lords can be appointed in different ways, including through a special commission.

The head of government is the prime minister, the leader of the party in power. The two dominant parties are the Conservatives and Labour.

The United Kingdom has access to oil reserves buried in the waters of the North Sea.

Economy

England is one of the richest countries in the world. Although it does not have many natural resources, the country is very advanced in industry and finance. England is the largest producer of aircraft in western Europe and **exports** many of its goods to the rest of the world. Its two biggest trading partners are Germany and the United States.

Agriculture is still an important part of the economy in England. Although very few people work in agriculture, English farms supply two-thirds of the country's needs thanks to modern farm machinery. The most important crops are barley and wheat. Potatoes, the staple food, are grown in large quantities. Dairy farming is important in England, too. Cows and sheep produce top-quality meats, milk and cheeses.

Dairy farming is a major industry in England. Many dairy farms are located in areas where there is heavy rainfall.

People and Lifestyle

People

The English population is a mixture of cultures, with **immigrants** arriving from all over the world. About 83 per cent of the population is **Caucasian**. **Minorities** form nearly 12 per cent of the population, with Asians making up the largest group, followed by West Indians and Africans.

England has a large immigrant community. These Asian migrants are workers at Borough Market in London.

To stand out from the crowd, this young woman has adopted the punk style, which usually features spiky, unusual hairstyles and clothes such as leather jackets.

The English people are very conscious of social classes. In the past, people from different classes did not mix often.

Family Life

English families tend to be small, with two or three children. Single-parent families are also becoming more common. Grandparents play an important role in child care, especially for single-parent families.

These grandparents read to their grandson before bedtime. Many grandparents play an important role in family life by helping to look after their grandchildren.

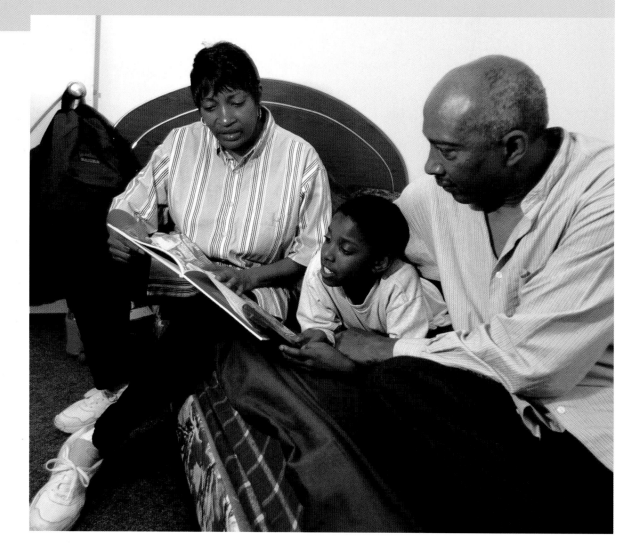

In 2007, England launched the National Youth Homelessness Scheme to help homeless young people living on the streets.

In many English homes, both parents need to work in order to contribute to the household and support the family. Others work because they enjoy their careers.

Teenage pregnancy is a problem in England. There are also concerns about homelessness and gang violence. Some people blame the break down of family life.

Education

Almost everybody in England can read and write. English children must go to school from age five to sixteen. When they are sixteen, students take examinations to decide if they should continue with school or get a job. Most of them leave school. Only one-quarter of the students continue their schooling for two more years and then enroll at a university to earn a **degree**.

A mother monitors her daughter's homework progress.

University of Portsmouth students celebrate Graduation Day, which falls in July every year.

English children enjoy many activities at school. Sports are very popular. Children play football, cricket, hockey, rugby, netball and gymnastics. Students also go on trips to see historical buildings, and even across the English Channel to France, where they practise speaking French.

Religion

In England, people enjoy freedom of religion. There are also schools that are linked to different faiths and where children receive both regular and religious education.

Nearly half of the English population belongs to the Church of England. Other major Christian denominations include Roman Catholic and Eastern Orthodox. Many other people practise Judaism, Buddhism and Islam.

St. Paul's Cathedral in London is one of the most famous Anglican churches in England.

The entire family gathers for Christmas dinner. On Christmas Day, people exchange cards and gifts and pull festive crackers.

The most important religious festival in England is Christmas. People attend church services and sing carols. They eat roast turkey and Christmas pudding, a traditional steamed pudding made with dried fruit. Many homes have a Christmas tree with pretty decorations and colourful lights.

Language

The English spoken in England today comes from Anglo-Saxon, a Germanic dialect, often called Old English. It also contains many words taken from Latin and French.

Geoffrey Chaucer (1343–1400) was one of the first authors to write in the common English that was spoken by the native people. He wrote *The Canterbury Tales.*

Literature

The first story in the English language was that of Beowulf, a brave hero. Other famous stories like *Frankenstein*, *Pride and Prejudice*, *Robinson Crusoe* and *A Tale of Two Cities* were all written by English authors.

English women started writing books in the eighteenth century. At first, writers like the Brontë sisters and Jane Austen used male names to hide the fact that they were women. Today, the most famous children's writer is J. K. Rowling, whose *Harry Potter* series is read by millions of children and adults alike.

In his novels, Charles Dickens (1812–1870) wrote about people in nineteenth-century England.

This ancient manuscript of the Anglo-Saxon poem *Beowulf* is believed to date from the tenth century. The work was written in Old English.

Arts

Painting

The Celts made beautiful jewellery and clothing from metals and precious stones. Warriors wore helmets and carried swords studded with gems.

The art of stained glass was very popular in England during the Middle Ages.

In London's **West End**, theatres abound. Theatre is one of England's most respected and accomplished art forms.

Later, English artists turned to sculpture and carving. They made beautiful statues in stone and carved objects in wood, ivory and bone. They also turned their attention to decorating houses with embroidered rugs and mats. Another important art form was the writing of script. Before the printing press was invented, books were written by hand and decorated with illustrations.

Modern Art

Two of the most well-known English painters are John Constable (1776–1837) and Joseph Turner (1775–1851). They both lived during the nineteenth century. Constable painted many scenes of the English countryside. Turner was famous for his landscapes and seascapes in watercolour.

Three Standing Figures is a stone artwork by renowned English sculptor Henry Moore (1898–1986) that adorns the grounds of Battersea Park in London.

Music

At the beginning of the twentieth century, Edward Elgar composed classical music while the team of Gilbert and Sullivan put on lively musicals. The most famous modern composer of musicals is Andrew Lloyd Webber. In the 1960s, the Beatles and the Rolling Stones became popular worldwide. Other musical groups from England that have achieved international success include Coldplay, The Verve and Snow Patrol.

In the early 1900s, the work of English composer Edward Elgar reflected England's prosperity.

Films

The English film industry has produced many magnificent films. The first English film star was Charlie Chaplin, who became famous worldwide for his slapstick brand of humour. A well-known English film hero is James Bond, who has been thrilling cinema-goers for more than forty years.

Daniel Day-Lewis, Helen Mirren and Rachel Weisz are English stars who have won Oscars since 2006. In 2009, the movie *Slumdog Millionaire* earned Danny Boyle two Oscars for Best Director and Best Picture. Actress Kate Winslet also won her first Oscar that year for her role in *The Reader*.

The **British Broadcasting Corporation (BBC)** produces excellent radio programmes and television documentaries.

Leisure Time

Many English people spend a lot of time in their gardens, planting and **pruning**. They are very proud of their colourful flowers and green lawns.

Punch and Judy shows began in the 1600s. They are still very popular with children. The characters were originally a pair of puppets: one called Punch and the other, his wife, Judy.

Many children watch television when they come home from school and at weekends.

Children like to read and watch television. When it is not raining, they like to play in the garden. One interesting game is called 'conkers'. Two players tie a horse chestnut (conker) to a string and take turns swinging at each other's chestnut until one conker cracks.

English families enjoy long walks in the countryside or along the rugged coastlines of England. Cycling and fishing are other popular hobbies.

Sports

England is a nation of sports lovers. The English invented many of the sports played today. Most students participate in sports and the country produces numerous world-class athletes.

The most popular sport in England is football. Boys compete with each other on school teams. Some girls play football, too. Professional football games attract large crowds at weekends.

Rowing is a popular university sport. The most famous rowing event in England is between Oxford and Cambridge universities and is known simply as The Boat Race.

Rugby season begins in September and ends in April with tournaments played throughout that time of the year.

Rugby is a sport played by many schoolboys. There are fifteen players to a team and the object of the game is to score points by running the ball to the end line. Rugby is played by kicking, side passing and dribbling the ball.

One sport in which England excels worldwide is hockey. Both the men's and women's hockey teams often win medals at the Olympics and at other international competitions.

Festivals

Many English festivals date from pre–Christian times. May Day is still celebrated as the first day of spring. Young girls dance around a **maypole** and Morris dancers perform folk dances in the streets.

Halloween began as a Celtic feast called Samhain. The Celts believed that the dead returned to life on that night.

Folk dancers known as Morris dancers perform on various occasions. They carry sticks and wear bells around their ankles.

People lit bonfires to keep evil spirits away and children played mischievous tricks. This was the origin of today's trick-or-treating.

In early spring comes Shrove Tuesday, or 'Pancake Day'. Lent starts the following day, traditionally a forty-day period of fasting. Today, some people give up favourite foods or bad habits. After Lent, on Easter Day, children search for chocolate eggs in their gardens.

On Guy Fawkes Night, on 5 November, people light bonfires and set off fireworks to mark the failed attempt to blow up parliament in 1605. Guy Fawkes was one of the plot's conspirators.

Started by the West Indian community in England, the Notting Hill Carnival draws crowds and participants from all over the world.

Food

Potatoes are eaten with many meals in England, together with meat and fresh vegetables. Fish and chips is a traditional English fast food. Chinese food, Indian curries and Middle Eastern kebabs are popular.

Children usually have lunch at school. This meal used to be high in fat but schools are changing to healthier foods.

Fish and chips are served with salt and vinegar and were traditionally wrapped in newspaper.

Sunday Lunch

Most families get together for Sunday lunch. A typical Sunday lunch would be roast beef, Yorkshire pudding, roast potatoes and vegetables. Some families meet at their local pub, which is a popular gathering place to eat lunch or dinner.

Funny Names

Some dishes have funny names. 'Bangers and mash' is sausages and mashed potatoes. 'Shepherd's Pie' is minced lamb and vegetables topped with mashed potatoes. Children also love 'toad-in-the-hole,' which is a dish of sausages baked in a tasty batter.

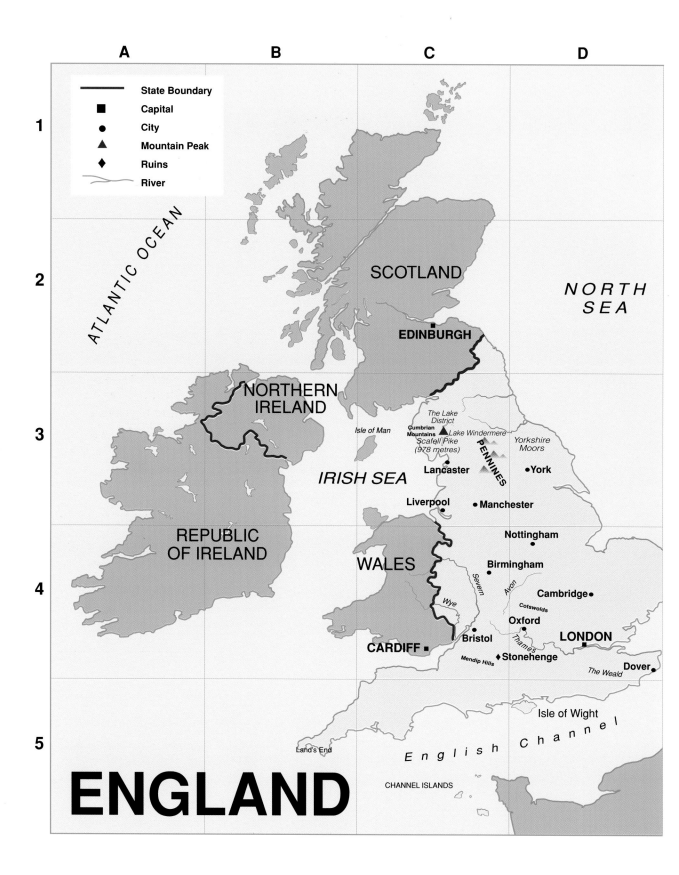

A · B · C · D

1
2
3
4
5

State Boundary
Capital
City
Mountain Peak
Ruins
River

ATLANTIC OCEAN

SCOTLAND

NORTH SEA

EDINBURGH

NORTHERN IRELAND

Isle of Man

The Lake District
Cumbrian Mountains
Scafell Pike
(978 metres)
Lake Windermere

PENNINES

Yorkshire Moors

Lancaster

York

IRISH SEA

Liverpool

Manchester

REPUBLIC OF IRELAND

Nottingham

WALES

Birmingham

Severn

Avon

Cambridge

Wye

Cotswolds

Oxford

LONDON

CARDIFF

Bristol

Thames

Mendip Hills

Stonehenge

The Weald

Dover

Isle of Wight

Land's End

English Channel

ENGLAND

CHANNEL ISLANDS

42

NORWAY

N

THE NETHERLANDS

•Calais BELGIUM

FRANCE

The rocky coastline of southwestern England.

Atlantic Ocean A2
Avon C4

Belgium E4
Birmingham C4
Bristol C4

Calais E5
Cambridge D4
Cardiff C4
Channel Islands C5
Cotswolds D4
Cumbrian
    Mountains C3

Dover D4

Edinburgh C2
English Channel
    C5–D5

France E5

Ireland, Republic of
    A4–B4
Irish Sea B3–C3
Isle of Man C3
Isle of Wight D5

Lake District C3
Lake Windermere C3
Land's End B5
Liverpool C3
London D4

Manchester C3
Mendip Hills C4

Netherlands, The E4
North Sea D2
Northern Ireland B3
Norway E1
Nottingham D3

Oxford D4

Pennines C3

Scafell Pike C3
Scotland C2
Severn River C4
Stonehenge C5

Thames D4

Wales C4
Weald, The D4
Wye River C4

York D3
Yorkshire Moors D3

Quick Facts

Official Name England (part of the United Kingdom)

Capital London

Official Language English

Population 51,446,000

Land Area 130,410 square kilometres

Highest Point Scafell Pike (978 metres)

Major Rivers Avon, Severn, Thames, Trent

Main Religion Church of England (often called Anglican)

Major Festivals Easter Day (varies), Halloween (31 October), Christmas (25 December)

Major Cities Birmingham, Leeds, Liverpool, Manchester, Sheffield

Head of State The monarch (Queen Elizabeth II as of 1952–though the country is ruled by parliament)

National Anthem 'God Save the Queen'

National Flag Cross of St. George

Currency Pound Sterling

The red double decker bus, Big Ben and the London Eye are three icons of London, England's capital city.

Glossary

annulled: to declare a marriage to have no legal existence

British Broadcasting Corporation (BBC): the official radio and television broadcaster of Great Britain

Caucasian: referring to people of European descent having similar physical characteristics, mainly light skin

Celts: a group of people who inhabited England and other parts of Europe. They had their own language, literature and religion.

Church of England: the church established by King Henry VIII. Also called the Anglican Church, it is the official church of the country.

colony: distant land that is governed by another country

Crusades: the various attempts by Christians in the late Middle Ages to take back Jerusalem from the Muslims

degree: a programme of study undertaken at a college or university

European Union: an economic and political organization consisting of 27 European countries

export: the process of selling and shipping products to other countries

immigrant: a person who moves to another country

invent: make or produce something for the first time

maypole: a pole with ribbons attached at the top. On May Day, young girls dance around the pole.

Middle Ages: the period of European history from 500 to 1500 CE

minorities: small cultural groups within a population

parliamentary monarchy: the system of government in which a country is ruled by elected politicians, with a king and/or queen as the symbolic head

pasture: an area of land used for grazing animals

patron saint: the protecting or guiding saint of a person or place

pruning: cutting off parts of a plant

Roman Empire: a large area of land mostly in Europe ruled by Rome from 27 BCE to the fifth century CE

social classes: groups with different levels of income and lifestyles

symbolic: representative of something

West End: an area in London famous for its theatres

For More Information

Books

Bailey, Jacqui. *Discover London*. London: Franklin Watts, 2008

Mayhew, James. *Katie and the British Artists*. London: Orchard Books, 2009

Murphy, Patricia J. *Let's Play Football*. DK Readers series. London: Dorling Kindersley Publishing, 2008

Reeves, James. *Stories from England*. Oxford Children's Myths and Legends series. Oxford: Oxford University Press, 2009

Wignall, Paul and Greenhill, Wendy. *Shakespeare's Theatre*. Shakespeare Library series. London: Heinemann Library, 2007

Yuan, Margaret Speaker. *The London Tower Bridge*. Building World Landmarks series. Michigan, USA: Cengage Gale, 2004

Tudor. Eyewitness series. London: Dorling Kindersley Publishing, 2008

DVDs

Globe Trekker: Ultimate England. (Pilot Productions, 2006).

Kings and Queens of England – Box-set. (Kultur Video, 2006).

Secrets in Stone: The Spirit of England. (Total-Content LLC, 2009).

Travel With Kids–England. (Equator Creative Media, 2008).

Visions of England. (Acorn Media, 2005).

Websites

www.britishlocalhistory.co.uk
Delve extensively into England's colourful history.

www.elizabethan-era.org.uk
Discover more about one of the most fascinating and greatest eras in England's royal courts.

www.england.mu
Read in-depth articles on the more unique side of England, such as castles and its football players.

www.visitbritain.com
Britain's official travel and tourism guide offers detailed city guides to get the reader better acquainted with the country.

Note to parents and teachers: Every effort has been made by the Publishers to ensure that these websites are suitable for children, that they are of the highest educational value, and that they contain no inappropriate or offensive material. However, because of the nature of the Internet, it is impossible to guarantee that the contents of these sites will not be altered. We strongly advise that Internet access is supervised by a responsible adult.

Index